T0156747

A SEARCH FOR *There*

STEPHEN J. KENNEDY

iUniverse, Inc.
Bloomington

A Search for There

Copyright © 2011 Stephen J. Kennedy

All rights reserved. No part of this book may be used or reproduced by any means, graphic, electronic, or mechanical, including photocopying, recording, taping or by any information storage retrieval system without the written permission of the publisher except in the case of brief quotations embodied in critical articles and reviews.

iUniverse books may be ordered through booksellers or by contacting:

iUniverse
1663 Liberty Drive
Bloomington, IN 47403
www.iuniverse.com
1-800-Authors (1-800-288-4677)

Because of the dynamic nature of the Internet, any Web addresses or links contained in this book may have changed since publication and may no longer be valid. The views expressed in this work are solely those of the author and do not necessarily reflect the views of the publisher, and the publisher hereby disclaims any responsibility for them.

Any people depicted in stock imagery provided by Thinkstock are models, and such images are being used for illustrative purposes only.

Certain stock imagery © Thinkstock.

ISBN: 978-1-4502-9376-1 (pbk)
ISBN: 978-1-4502-9378-5 (cloth)
ISBN: 978-1-4502-9377-8 (ebk)

Printed in the United States of America

iUniverse rev. date: 4/5/2011

CONTENTS

Note to the Reader

Once upon a time, I decided to do something. And I did it. The decision was to leave the Roman Catholic priesthood. The doing was in April 1966. Hard upon this decision and the doing came a further decision: the decision to leave Christianity and all organized religion. These decisions and the doing opened a door into a center within me—a living center whose point reaches unto the *beginning*!

Before leaving the priesthood, I was asked to write a letter to Rome explaining why I wanted a "leave of absence." I gave the request some thought, and I wrote the following brief letter:

> I have decided to leave the priesthood
> because I do not want to be *here*. By *here*,
> I mean existing and moving about in this huge
> structure, framework, way of life.
> What I really want is to be *there*.
> By *there*, I mean an open field where I
> may discover *who I am!*

I was told that the letter was too brief and it gave no clear explanation as to why I was leaving. I was asked to write another letter. I refused because what I wrote was exactly what I felt inside. I could not explain what the "there" meant or the nature of the "open field" because only the "leaving" and the searching would reveal that.

What I did know with certainty within a year of leaving was that I did not want to find my identity by being a member of any group.

A Search For There is not a history. It is not a description of a sequence of events. It is an attempt to describe what I call "happenings," things that occur that were not planned or in any way expected.

The four main parts as set out in the table of contents—Leaving, Myth, Question, and Dialogue—were not written in that order. In brief comments on each part, I provide, where necessary, a historical context of events. I also discuss certain words, images, and symbols to describe the happenings.

In his play *The Family Reunion*, T. S. Eliot has one of his characters say:

> But how can I explain, how can I explain to you?
> You will understand less after I have explained it.
> All that I could hope to make you understand
> Is only events; not what has happened.
> And people to whom nothing has ever happened
> Cannot understand the unimportance of events.[1]

What Eliot writes may well be so, but what I am attempting through words, images, and symbols is not to explain but to touch within you a cord that binds us all and reaches unto a beginning. It is in this spirit I share with you my search for there.

COMMENTS ON LEAVING

The literal meaning of "leaving" is a moving from a "here" to a "there." Both the "here" and the "there" are crucial in that every leaving is a taking-with. We see this in the prototype of all human leaving: leaving the womb.

Every leaving creates its own particular "there." In most cases, analogous to my leaving, it is a matter of leaving one group and becoming part of another. When I left the Catholic priesthood, I was still a Catholic but not a priest. However, when I left Christianity and all organized religion, what was the meaning of the "there" I created?

Searching for an answer to this question, I was drawn into a strange space where inside and outside were one—a oneness urging me to begin at the moment of being and let it develop from there.

Leaving—
A Primal Form of Search

Leaving?

The leaving
Is the leaving of
Proto-Womb-Leaving
Creat*ing* *outside*
inside be*ing* *joy*
In the presence of
There.

In the Beginning

The Moment of Being

I have no memory of my beginning. And yet, I did have a beginning.

Beginning suggests time. At some point in time, I began to exist. Can I find the point? The individual existent!

In the beginning, there appears to be no memory. For try as I may, I cannot remember becoming one cell. That unforgettable yet amnesiac moment of ecstasy. That almost timeless second of the egg-sperm/sperm-egg union appears and vanishes without a trace.

"'Tis here, 'Tis Here, 'Tis Gone." And surely I "do it wrong, being so majestical" to dare to presume to confine in my time this ghost of mother and father. No memory of the first ecstasy.

The egg and sperm truly stood outside themselves, an ex-stasis. They lost themselves without trace to become me. Yes, without trace, no memory of the former times of egg and sperm existence. That restless driving search to be one—a force like the nuclear.

And yet, at times I hear the ghostlike murmur, the whisper, of a half-mother and a half-father locked within the castle of my every cell.

The murmur, the whisper, are a hint of memory, the memory of the-timeless-oneness-of-a-unique-half-mother-and-a-unique-half-father-who-searched-and-found-each-other-*be*ing* me.

Spontaneously I cry out: "O day and night, but this is wondrous strange!"

In reply, I sense an invitation to a oneness and hear a silence saying: "And therefore as stranger give it welcome ..."

and ...

I do.

Memory

The beginning appears to be the point of being one cell and only one cell. Each half has forgotten the past, becoming one in a timeless moment.

But is this really the beginning?

My beginning, all beginning is in time. And all time has memory. Time proceeds from memory as from a point. For the point is the mystery called *life*.

My beginning then is twofold. My first beginning is without my memory. It is my existence at the moment of oneness, just prior to the impulse of memory.

It was the memory in the egg and sperm that sent them in search of one another. It is now in my time, my second beginning, that the memory of the one cell (it now stands in itself, and its two halves are one) remembers that it can be two, and the two, four and the four, eight and the eight, ... and so on and so on.

All this I remember very clearly.

Discovering *W a l l*

In the beginning, there is silence in a rhythm of darkness. The poetry, the music of *l i f e*. My first *w a l l* is not made of stones. It is living flesh.

I am w a l l e d about and by myself but not alone. I divide and divide in perfect rhythm with my friend, the ever-beating drum.

Soon I begin to swim, and I love it, holding my breath forever. I swim and divide and never come to the surface.

Where did this living universe come from?

Where is its point?

What "immortal hand" or force "did frame"

This living universe?

Such questions—being words, not silence—do not exist. The walled-world of living flesh is beyond my world. I know no *w a l l s*!

One day, however, I experience the first inkling. I sense that my dividing is getting me into trouble. The trouble is twofold: First, I am now frequently running into a t h i n g! Second, there is no room to dive, and I can barely do two strokes on my back. I am still adept at holding my breath, and I cock my ears constantly to the soothing rhythm of the ever-beating drum.

Now that I can no longer swim, I devise a clever plan of exercises:

1. I turn quickly from my back to my stomach;
2. I kick out wildly at this t h i n g;
3. And when I rest on my back in stillness, I suck my thumb.

Of the three exercises, it is the kicking that gives me my first insight into the meaning of the thing called "being-walled-in." It is a glimpse into the meaning of the silent oneness of inside and outside, of here and there, and so on, and so on, into the roots of all knowing.

With each new kick, there is a growing awareness that if I am walled-in, there is a way-out.

There is a *d o o r.*

Discovering D o o r

Every now and then, I have the following dream:

I am descending a winding stone stairway in an old castle. As I move down the stairway, it becomes smaller and smaller ... until eventually I am crouching ... then crawling ... then I am on my belly moving very slowly. Finally I am stuck. There is only one way out ... forward. I can't quite make it... I wake up.

I know when I wake up that I did get out. With a sudden start, I also learn that this new world is full of shocks. As I shoot with a shock to the surface, I begin to breathe reluctantly, innately knowing I will have to go on breathing almost forever.

My first awareness reveals a world infinitely more vast than my first world ... where I learned to swim, dive, hold my breath forever ... the world of darkness, rhythm, and silence ... the world of my friend and comforter, the ever-beating drum.

As I stretch out naked, cold, alone, I sense immediately there are no w a l l s.

A world without walls is surely paradise.

I begin to cry and cry with near infinite delight. Those about me attempt to comfort me, for they have no inkling as to the source of my *j o y be*ing a*glimpse* into the unending *o p e n n e s s of my new world.*

Comments on Myth

After I left the priesthood, I was employed by the Ontario government as a probation officer. I also began working on a degree in psychology, attending night classes at the University of Windsor. In July 1967, Barbara and I were married; and by 1972, we had three children. In 1973, I completed my degree in psychology and decided to study law. So in the years 1974 to 1979, while studying law and completing the requirements to be admitted to the bar in Ontario, I had time to read, write, and listen. I wrote a manuscript of 110 pages with the title *Peter, Where Are You?* I later changed the title to *Stephen, Where Are You?* It was my first attempt to answer the question: What is the meaning of the "there" I created when I left Christianity and all organized religion? This manuscript was revised from time to time, and eventually, in a greatly reduced form, it became the part I call myth.

Myth is divided into two parts: "The Meaning of Driftwood" and "The Marvelous Labyrinth of Love." The page "The Letter from Barbara" (written in 1976) is a remnant of the early manuscript. The words and images in this letter (as strange as it may appear to the reader) reached into and touched a transformation that was taking place inside me—the awareness of a growing inner freedom and a transforming perspective flowing from it.

The two pieces of driftwood are a metaphor of my eyes. No matter what "world" one is born into and grows and develops in, that "world" shapes one's "eyes" and gives one a unique perspective. The words I heard as an infant and a child and learned to speak—the symbols, gestures, teachings concerning the meaning of life, death, and so on—shaped my eyes and gave me the perspective of the "here" I described in my letter to Rome—a "here" that I decided to leave so I could find a "field," find a "there" that would give me a transforming perspective.

Myth—
A Primal Form of Search

Myth!

In the writing of my life (in its inner/outer happenings and events), I was led, and at times driven, to write my own "myth." All of us living on this planet can in levels of our being and consciousness, and to some extent historically, connect our roots to a tribe or tribes. And "In archaic societies," as Mircea Eliade writes in *Myth and Reality*, "Myth means a true story and, beyond that is a most precious possession because it is sacred, exemplary, and significant."[2]

Each of us, from the root and gift of our beginning in a union of a unique half-mother and a unique half-father, and with a capacity for the happening of consciousness, is *sacred, exemplary,* and *significant.*

A Letter from Barbara

Stephen, I am here. I miss you. Today I had the strangest sensation; and it urges me now, this evening, to write to you.

Crossing the pavement with the groceries, I tripped in a drain. In the fall and confusion, I forgot for the moment where you were and even who you are. It was as if I was torn apart and healed in the same instant and left with only a vague and improbable feeling of loss.

Someone helped me to my feet, and soon I was moving as before in the blue-gray pattern that is our way.

THE MEANING OF DRIFTWOOD

One

In a village, on the coast, Stephen was born. It was a bright Tuesday morning near the end of September.

The mist had lifted, leaving the black cliffs steaming in the morning sun. Miles away, someone was plowing a field. Flocks of gray gulls were feeding on the furrows.

The mother bled. She was weak. She smiled faintly at the wrinkled form held before her, lightly glowing like a faint star.

As she slept, she sensed the gulls swarm and feed on the plowed earth.

That morning, miles away, a lady sat on the marble sill of a window. Below her and stretching out to the cliffs were meadows and pastures. Beyond the cliffs was the sea. She sat still, her eyes skimming the heads of the sheep to the sea.

For years the lady had been a source of wisdom and counsel in the village. Talk forced her to leave the village shortly before Stephen was born. Her whereabouts were a secret.

Stephen's mother had gone to the lady with Stephen in her womb. Gently, the lady laid her hands on the rounded belly. She said, "The child will be a fine healthy boy."

The mother flushed and, beaming thanks, stirred to leave, but the lady held her hands cupped on the bulging skirt. The mother waited.

"From the beginning, he will be open to the world. At first, the world will be as fragments. Then, slowly, he will listen and learn to see."

Two

Rocks, gray-black rocks, were Stephen's earliest memories.

The rocks are huge … as big as half a house. Some are worn smooth and round, and we would arch over them and lie still, rubbing the smoothness with flat hands.

Down at the cove, there are big jagged rocks. Stephen would go down there and throw crusts to the gulls. Once he cut his foot there, and the blood came and came.

"Put it in a cold spring," said one of the boys.

So we searched for a pool of clear, cold water.

"Let's dig one!"

With pieces of driftwood, we scraped away at the coarse brown sand. Soon the cold water bubbled up, and we supported the walls with flat stones.

A few days later, Stephen came back, and the spring was half full of sand. He cleaned out the sand and put heavier stones on the walls. He kept it clear and open all that summer.

*

One morning when Stephen was a boy, he awoke very early. Dressing quietly in the dark, he left the house and climbed down the mist-wet rocks to the sea. The brown sand was thick and heavy with salt spray.

He followed the edge of the tide until the sun was up and then turned homeward. Lulled by the rush and ebb of the tide, he was oblivious to the three gray gulls circling and diving around him, screeching out for crusts.

Suddenly he stopped. There in front of him, half covered by the new-formed sand, were two pieces of driftwood born of the tide. Bending down, he plucked them carefully from their moist sandy sockets and carried them home.

When he opened the door of the back kitchen, his parents turned from their breakfast to greet him.

"There's himself!" said his father, leaning back on his chair.

"And where has our wandering Aegnus been at so early an hour?" smiled his mother, drinking tea from a saucer.

"Look! Just look what I found!"

Stephen brushed the sand off into the wood box and placed the two pieces of driftwood before his parents.

The father picked them up and examined them carefully. Stephen followed the movement of his father's eyes and hands, straining to absorb the discoveries. The father turned the pieces in his hands, measuring with his eyes their form and weighing them with his mind.

Stephen stood entranced.

All the while, the mother attended Stephen's eyes.

"There," said the father abruptly, laying the driftwood on the table. "They're a pair! Yes, sir, they're a pair!" And he pursed his lips in wisdom.

Stephen's mouth was open.

"Close your mouth, Stephen, and wash up for breakfast," said his mother with a smile on her lips.

Stephen picked up the two pieces of driftwood and turned to her. "What do you think?"

"Well ... there are three in all, Stephen, three. But you will find the third ... I'm sure you will. Now leave them with me and go wash up for breakfast."

Later that day, Stephen sought out his mother. She was busy in the kitchen, and the pieces of driftwood were sitting in front of the fire.

"And why are they before the fire?"

"So the green of the sea can dry into the soft white wood. That's important, Stephen. It's important not to lose any of the green."

"What will I do with them when they are dry?"

"They're special, Stephen, rare and special. So I feel when you are of age, you should take them and show them to the lady."

Three

The village where Stephen was born is similar to many villages along the coast. In fact, it is similar to many villages all over the earth. It houses two or three thousand people born into traditions and beliefs; surviving from goods of sea and land; satisfied, more or less, with a thin crust of an immediate past; convinced, not in their beliefs but in their souls, that time is a box where they are buried.

A highway runs through the village. Going west, it leads to the market town and beyond to the city. In the east, it passes near an old monastery in the foothills. In the mountains is the well-known upper valley, which has been a source of legend and myth. Within the circumference of the mountains and the market town, Stephen grew up.

One of the livelihoods in the village is the cultivation and harvesting of laver. The laver industry is owned by the Dixon family. The summer Stephen was seventeen, he went to work for the Dixons.

"Yes," Stephen's dad said one day in early summer, "I spoke to Jack Dixon; and he said, 'Sure, send him over and we'll put him to work.'"

Jack's father had built up a profitable business with his lush crops of algae. He was a shrewd, hardheaded man.

As a lad, Jack went off to boarding school and came home with a head full of poems. He had a quick tongue, and his wry humor won him a reputation. The summer he finished boarding school, he was over at the alehouse one day drinking himself stiff with celebration. Suddenly he jumped up on a table and began to recite poetry and to dance. He was ordered down, but would not go without a scrap.

He caught hell from Mr. Dixon, who had no pity for his broken nose.

"You'll get serious or get out," said Mr. Dixon.

Jack decided to get out and go to the city. But before the summer was out, Mr. Dixon had a stroke, which left him with a speech problem and a paralysis of his right side.

Jack never wanted the business. His father's eyes begged him, and Jack succumbed out of pity—but he would do it his way. Now, five years later, Stephen came to work for him.

The Dixon property is at the edge of the village. Here the cliffs dip, forming several plateaus down to the beach. A series of wooden steps connect the levels. At the lowest level, there is a long storage shed and an office. It was here that Stephen reported for work.

"There you are, Stephen," said Jack, coming out of the office. "Put your lunch pail in there and come with me. I'll show you what we're doing."

In the office near a desk sat Mr. Dixon. Stephen had not seen him since his stroke. He remembered him as a formidable man, a man who had chased them on the beach as children.

"Get away from my works," he would say, "or I'll take a stick to you all." And he would.

Stephen slipped inside the door and put down his lunch pail. Mr. Dixon glanced at him, his mouth contorted, his limp right arm rocking back and forth. Stephen shivered. Here was not the daylight Mr. Dixon who chased him with a stick on the beach; here was some dark, half-hidden presence with power to half-swallow a body. He greeted the man quickly and left the office.

Jack and Mr. Dixon were forever at war. The father hovered in the background, trying to direct with his painful speech and the gestures of his good left arm. Jack would look up and there he was, dragging his reluctant right leg across the beach, his face twisted with paresis and frustration. But Jack stood his ground; and in the end, the father turned away, muttering with bitter anger.

Stephen followed Jack down the wooden steps and across the sand to the drying racks. Jack, tall and loose-limbed, talked on constantly, turning to Stephen to mock him with his eyes.

"So you're big enough to work now, are you?... Good God, and it's a sad day. It'll be the end of your exploring now, won't it? By God, those were the days, aye, Stephen?"

He stopped and turned around. "Just look!" he said, gesturing toward the mile or two of beach down to the cove. "Just look. God's own forest of rock and sand ... why, one could spend their life just there, in those few miles of rounded rock."

Jack gave a shrug and walked to the racks in silence.

The summer passed quickly, with Stephen falling into a harness of chores. He helped here and there, to repair, to carry, to be on hand. Often he worked side by side with Jack, forming a sort of backup crew. Several other men in Jack's hire had more regular jobs connected directly with the cultivation of the algae on the long nets stretched out in the shallow water.

As the weeks passed, Jack liked to have Stephen near him. He found in Stephen a sensitive foil.

"You're doing fine, lad," said Jack one day, eyeing Stephen with a cynical smile. "Aye, in a few months you've become near an expert!" He laughed, watching Stephen closely.

"I'm catching on," said Stephen.

"Would you like to make it a career?" Jack asked mockingly.

31

"I like it," said Stephen, returning his look, "but not as a career. I'm not suited for it."

"Not suited?" laughed Jack. "Have you thought about it that much? Most around here don't think at all. They fall into a niche, squirm a bit, then lie until they die."

He paused and looked away from Stephen to where several men were piling ripe algae into carts.

"I won't mock your thinking," said Jack in a softer tone. "The summers when I was fresh home from boarding school, I would spend days on the beach, climbing the big rocks. It all seemed so new and different after months away. The clean sharp smell of salt and seaweed; the constant murmur of the sea. I had forgotten how the sea is never silent. And those rocks so big and mysterious, to lie over the round ones, reaching your hand down to where it was cool, dark, and damp away from the sun. Some days I would have so many thoughts, feel so full of wisdom.

"Then my dad would come out of the office and see me down on the beach, just lying there. He would shout to come and lend a hand; and before I was halfway up the steps, he would ask, 'What are you doing there anyway?'

"'Oh, I was just thinking,' I would tell him.

"And he would give a shrug and go into the office saying, 'Leave the thinking to those who can. Come on now and lend a hand.'"

There were many such conversations mingled with the joking and mocking. Stephen sensed a sadness in the man, a carefully hidden sadness.

"Oh, come now, Stephen," said his mother. "There's no sadness in Jack. Why, he's a keen, lively, young man. You should have seen him at the house party just two weeks ago. He certainly likes his liquor, but he's so much fun. He had us in stitches over and over. It's probably you that are the sad one, with your thinking about things too much. But poets can't help it, can they?" she said quickly, giving him her warmest smile.

"No, I don't think it's me. It's something that came spontaneously, from inside, without any thinking ... in images. Well anyway, I'd better be off, or I'll be late."

She saw him to the door. "What images, Stephen?"

"Oh, like something broken, yes, like something broken."

There was a rabbit Stephen and his brother Bill had snared once in the endless miles of woods near the village. Just the paw was caught in the biting picture wire. The rabbit pulled and pulled, peeling back the fur, the raw muscle, finally snapping the bone. It ran away, free, on its bleeding stump.

Four

The village where Stephen grew up is different from many villages along the coast. In fact, it is different from many villages all over the earth. What makes the difference is the spirit of place. That living blend of traditions and custom that gives its own shape to the consciousness of our growing years. Bluntly, but marvelously described by Michael de Montaigne:

> For truly, Custome is a violent and deceiving schoole-mistris. She by little and little, and as it were by stealth, establisheth the foot of her authoritie in us; by which mild and gentle beginning, if once by the aid of time, it have setled and planted the same in us, it will soone discover a furious and tyrannicall countenance unto us, against which we have no more the libertie to lift so much as our eies.[3]

A focus in the village is the alehouse. It sits off the highway in the center of the village on a hill. Down the hill from the alehouse are the charred, black-gray ruins of a house. The house was burned to the ground by an angry mob some years before Stephen was born. The owner, a man in his forties, was in the house and was burned with it. Whether this was or was not the intent of the mob is not clear. But even more uncertain and fogged over is the story of a green pony. Rumor had it that the man had a green pony, and it lived with him in the house.

To the outsider, the modern man, standing square and silent in his city, stories of green ponies are a pleasure. But not here in the village so close to the upper valley and the mountains.

The September Stephen was nineteen, he decided to leave home. He would travel and study.

Jack was sorry to see him leave.

"I'll miss you," said Jack, "but there you go. What's to be done?" He stammered a little looking for words. "Well ... we'll have to send you off right though. It's over to the alehouse with you and a good solemn drink."

They both laughed.

Stephen soon fell way behind Jack in the drinking bout. Mug after mug settled quietly in Jack's belly.

"Do you see old Fergus over there?" asked Jack, pointing a relatively steady finger to an old man seated alone by a green window.

"A strange man," said Stephen.

"Yes, if by strange you mean crazy." Jack laughed loudly.

Fergus was renowned in the village. Called by a few an eccentric, but by most an idiot. No one knew his age. The old ones said, "He's over sixty, you know." But nobody knew for sure.

Fergus begged and also did odd jobs. He lived by himself in a lean-to. He was like one of those early monks who left all and went out into the Egyptian desert just to be alone with their God and the ever-shifting sands.

Fergus sat there now, motionless, staring through the green window. Through the window just down the hill, one could see the charred ruins of the burned house.

Stephen helped Jack home, lodging him carefully inside the door. Walking home in the dark, he was relaxed, eager for tomorrow. He wanted to leave. The village was closing in on him, not so much in his thoughts as in his feelings.

A new moon bent down over the mountains. Stephen watched it as he walked along the edge of the highway into the village.

He thought of the driftwood. Those two pieces of white-green wood, tossed upon the beach, almost perfectly identical, like two strange, green-white eyes … hidden eyes. He would often hold them, studying them quietly with his fingers. They were always near the edge of his awareness, a sort of beacon, a focus for his emerging feelings.

There are so many bits and pieces in life … here and there, moving, the past, the present, the future … the old men. Stephen would often see the old men in the streets or near the alehouse, talking together, leaning on sticks, shifting their bodies with great care, laughing softly with their eyes … the resilience gone from their cheeks.

"Things have somehow to be put together" was a frequent saying; and the old men's eyes would smile, and sometimes they spit as they said it.

Perhaps he would seek out the lady and bring the driftwood to her. Yes, he would do that first.

His parents encouraged him at breakfast, talking on and on, giving directions, pointers, arguing among themselves, reconciling, laughing tightly, pouring more tea into near-full cups.

His mother had some information on how he might contact the lady, and she repeated it over and over.

Stephen was ready. His mother kissed him warmly, loving him with moist eyes. His father gave him a big hug and kissed him on the lips.

They ushered him out of the door with long waves and nervous smiles. The mother shouted across the white picket gate down the dusty lane, "Remember the marketplace first." The father fidgeted in the doorway, looking from side to side into the empty morning, mumbling, "Hold your voice down, woman, and let the boy be."

The mother came back from the gate holding an apron in her hands. The father, guilty over his reproach, guided her into the house with a tender arm. "He'll be fine, you'll see, you'll see," he said in half a whisper.

Five

The highway running west out of the village follows the coast for a number of miles in a near-straight line. Then a sharp elbow of rock sends it north, where it eventually follows the river west again into the town. The elbow forms a natural break with the village and its terrain. At this point, the land drops in a series of hills until it reaches the low plateau of the town.

Stephen repeated his mother's instructions: go to the marketplace, find the Quark Inn, ask how to contact the lady.

As he rounded the elbow and made the repeated rise-descent-rise-descent to the town, the instructions—the whole quest—sounded unreal, flat. By the time the din of the market was in the distance, he determined to sell the driftwood and be done with it.

Nearing the outskirts of the market, he saw clusters of young men puffing cigarettes and cheap pipes, their caps cocked back. They poked at one another in jest, making faces at things said, and sending short laughs into the sky. While they jousted, their eyes watched women hurrying into the thick crowd.

To Stephen, edging his way into the square, the young men were everywhere—in lanes, by stone walls, in clumps on corners—the stout seed oozing from images in their eyes.

The marketplace sang with a hum of having faces. Faces soothing one another with a mixture of masks, turning tongues around eyes in a screw of own.

Crowding in among flora and fauna, shrubs piled high, lamb carcasses laid on pine crates, they handled the turnips for size and soundness. Cutting through hot smell of he-goats, sheep urine, droppings of ducks and wild turkeys, they eyed with care neat rows of gutted fish. On they went elbowing, bolting by red-backed sandpipers caged in wire, to glass tanks of green piranha, bottled pirate spiders, beautiful pitcher plants. On and on in a driven circle, sawdust and dung making organic paste on their soles.

Off this crowded square, here and there, behind curtains and canvas shutters, came sighs of goat-songs, whimpers, shrill laughter, belly gurgles as the ice shifted, floundering in the clink of glasses on warm stone lips.

Stephen held the symmetrical pieces of white-green wood in bargain before many faces, but received only smiles, shrugs, the offer of apples. One old woman held a shining coin to his nose, the price of an apple. Stephen put the driftwood back into the brown paper bag. In despair, he let himself be bumped along by bodies.

Thus he rounded the driven circle several times before plucking himself free into a doorway.

"What can we do for you, lad?" A stout man in an apron studied Stephen with large immobile eyes.

"I'm looking for the Quark Inn," Stephen replied, unnerved by the eyes.

"The Quark?" The stout one laughed in a shout, spinning his neck from side to side without moving his eyes.

"Did you hear that, you wet-nosed lackeys? The Quark!" And he spun his neck to four pinched-nosed men seated just inside the door. They were lined up before four porcelain steins, from which they drank weakly, gratis—the chorus of the stout one.

Lifting their steins, they spoke as one:

"Aye, aye,
The Quark,
The misty Inn of memory.
Traffic in spice tums,
Frankincense, fragrant resins, and gums—
The fossil no eye has seen."

Taking a long weak drink, they sat quietly on the plank bench.

"There you have it, lad. The Quark is but a memory in this market. Surely it did exist at one time, but not at this time. But no harm done, lad. What the Quark did, we can do. The Owl at your service."

The owl, predator of small animals, especially rodents; wise, because its eyes encased in bony sockets do not move. Stephen observed this stuffed bird and his wide, bulging eyes and long talons ... but he was weary, a harried field mouse somewhere in the grasses.

"I'll come in and sit awhile."

"Good lad," said the Owl, rubbing his apron.

Stephen sat away from the chorus at a clean plank table.

"Well then, what will it be?"

"Laver grilled on toast and cider."

The Owl shouted the order to some back room and then hovered near the table, speaking down to Stephen in grins.

"You're wise. Do you know where laver grows best?"

"In nitrogen-rich water."

"Right, which is found near sewage outlets."

"Not only! The sea, like our lives, is full of waste."

"Ho! Ho! A young scholar!"

The owl spun his neck to the chorus. They raised their steins:

> "Laver is rich food
> Grown on our waste;
> And that is why it had
> An oyster-like taste."

Stephen ate the reddish algae, helping it down with pepper and vinegar. It lacked the body and texture of the lush pink algae harvested near home. But the cider was mellow and strong.

"More cider for the lad."

Stephen drank well into the second glass and sat back in a spin.

"What did you want with the Quark, lad?"

"I hoped to find out where the lady lives."

"The lady!"

"Yes, the lady."

"Who is this lady?"

"I don't know. I just know she's special, and I want to show her two pieces of driftwood I found."

"Aye, what you have in the bag there. I saw you hug it like treasure. Could I have a look?"

Stephen placed the driftwood on the table.

"They're indeed fine. A brilliant pair. Maybe I can help you. If anyone knows about special people, the woodcarver does. Drink your cider and have another on me. Then I'll tell you how to get to the woodcarver.

"Now the thing to remember when you arrive at the woodcarver's and the huge servant comes to the door is: to stand a cocky stance! The woodcarver is out to those who can't stand up to that huge, ugly servant of his. Off you go, lad!"

"Good luck! Good luck!" cried the chorus.

Six

Stephen walked deliberately down the straight street, putting each foot forward carefully, as one hell-bent on getting his sea legs. His outward form was molded armor, all the more to hold the hot liquid of his soul. He fixed the Trojan horse in his eye. In his hand was the crusader's two-edged sword; he brought it down from time to time on a cringing head.

Opening the black iron gate, crossing the gravel path as in a dream, knocking solidly on the carved oak door ...

The huge servant appeared ... glacial eyes, down-warping lids, tundra-stubbled face, crustal uplifted chin, a mouth of unsorted rock rubble ... a creature more figment than fact. Yet he stood there, grim, real as a broken branch.

"*W e l l*?" he roared in echoes.

Stephen's thin eyes remembered. Stand a cocky stance. But his soul was churned butter. In anguish, he pained to bring forth a word ...

Verbum, verbum, verbum.

A powerful infinite *w o r d*! A *word* at once Logos and Ergon.

The ...

Word*deed*word?

But alas! The marketplace muddled his memory. The edge of his mind was crowded with clichés, ... such as ...

"I'm from the tax department."

"I'm a messenger of the king."

"I'm the son of God."

He turned on his heel and ran.

Out of breath, he stumbled onto the grass near a tall birch. His heart continued to bound on in wild escape, his temples pounding with blood and booze.

He bent his head on his knees, closed his eyes, and gripped himself tightly together—opening his eyes from time to time to stop the spinning ... drifting off into dream ...

Running wildly on bog reeds, and cuckoo flowers whipping his legs; pitching forward onto soft sponge, lying quietly among reed and wild, ragged robins ...

Lifting his head, he saw a vestal arranging a bouquet of ragged robins in a black-figured vase.

Showing him a full nymph face, she asked, "Have you ever experienced it?"

She then showed him a statue-still profile with exquisite, long, curved neck and chin, the perfect bittern imitating reeds and grasses.

"Well?" she whispered in soft echoes.

Silence.

Softness of tone; faint perfume of ragged robins swaying in reeds; mirrored neck and chin, stirring up l o n g w a v e s of pink and white b i t t e r r o o t.

His dry tongue stumbled over the word, then gave up. It came of itself. "Black bottom jazz."

He repeated it. "Black bottom jazz. Black …"

With increasing volume. "Black bottom *jazz*."

With increasing confidence, it rolled off his tongue like Burbage: "Inky cloak … inky cloak … good mother … good mother …"

"*G o o d.*" She spoke, bending her full face to him—an aged face, a tenderly aged face, with slight traces of vestal on the forehead and tiny nooks of nymph near her mouth and chin—her eyes, not a linger of yeast.

"*G o o d*, you are very close. The word is *b l a c k h o l e*. The foundering star in a final ecstasy falls freely into itself, leaving wholly darkness."

Stephen woke cold and wet from the soft rain. Armed with the word, he set off with clear head and confidence to meet the woodcarver.

The black iron gate was open. The gravel path rolled smooth. Holding up the weighted brass knocker, he let it fall against the oak.

The huge servant appeared. At once the servant knew that he knew the word, and everybody was laughing, just a little.

So the servant didn't say, "*W e l l?*"

But, "Good day, young man."

And Stephen knew that he knew the word was not to be said, so he didn't say: "*b l a c k h o l e.*"

But, "I've come to see the woodcarver."

Seven

Stephen followed the huge servant into the sitting room, a long, spacious room with a wide stone fireplace. The walls were full wood, tongue and groove. The dark oak beams and the deep, square, carved and covered furniture gave the room a presence of hidden power.

On the polished writing desk sat a rough wooden carving of a monk kneeling and reading. The gaunt face was lined with unspeakable grimness.

The woodcarver stood up as they entered: a tall, trim man whose shortish hair served to fire the austerity of his eyes and smooth cheeks. He would not have his solitude easily intruded upon.

He was a man of great skill. A man, they said, with a vision—a man who portrayed in wood the profound and somber absurdity of life.

"You wish to see me!" The woodcarver glanced at the huge servant.

"Sir, I think you may want to spend a few moments with the young man."

"Very well, Anu," said the woodcarver. He trusted the huge servant implicitly.

Anu nodded and left the room.

"Sit down, young man," said the woodcarver.

They sat in square, black, leather chairs facing one another. The woodcarver waited. Stephen began speaking slowly.

"My name is Stephen. I was told that you may know where the lady lives. I would like to meet her and show her two pieces of driftwood. I found them a few years ago on the beach, born of the tide."

As he spoke, Stephen took the driftwood from the brown paper bag.

"Let me see them," said the woodcarver.

He took the pieces and sat back, taking a long time to study them.

"On the beach, you say?"

"Yes sir, I found them on the beach."

"Tell me how you found them."

Stephen told him how he woke very early one morning, climbed down to the beach, and so on.

"Washed in by the tide, you say?"

"Yes sir, I believe so."

"I see ... I see ..."

A long pause.

"Has anyone told you what they are?" asked the woodcarver.

"No sir, but most sense something rare, something special about them."

A pause.

"They are," said the woodcarver, "a near-perfect work of art."

"Yes," said Stephen, "near-perfect. But there is something missing."

"Missing?"

"I feel there is. Something has to be added—or found—so they may speak what they really are."

"Indeed?" smiled the woodcarver. "What they really are?" His smile loosened the harshness of his lips. "I agree and disagree," he said, flashing his eyes from the pieces to Stephen and back to the pieces. "Indeed, something has to be added. And it will, by you. Just as it was once by me. But adding is infinite. No, they will never speak what they are."

Abruptly the woodcarver stood up and went to the fireplace.

"Do you know why?" he continued, his back to Stephen.

"No, sir."

"Because they are a nothing," he said solemnly, still holding his back to Stephen. "That is why we can go on adding to them, because they are a nothing."

For some moments the woodcarver stared into the empty grate. Then he turned to Stephen and asked, "Do you understand me?"

"No, sir."

"Very well," he said and sat down. "Now I will tell you where the lady lives. Follow the highway west toward the city. Some miles this side of the city, there is a turning to your left that will take you to a large, sprawling structure on the coast. There, in that structure, off one of the many corridors, the lady lives."

Stephen stood up. "Thank you, sir," he said.

In silence, Anu showed Stephen out.

Eight

Stephen entered the large, sprawling structure on the coast in the September he turned nineteen. He walked the corridors for nearly thirteen years. One day near the end of his twelfth year, he was in one of the corridors vaguely in search of the lady. Suddenly coming toward him was a strange sound.

The sound of sandals came before him. Three monks approached Stephen in the dim corridor. The round one in the middle had the face of Mars; his mouth and chin were his own. Two wiry satellites flanked him; their ears were borrowed.

"Good day. You seem to be lost," said the round one to Stephen.

"I was told that off one of the corridors the lady lives."

"The lady!"

"Yes, the lady."

"I have never seen the lady. And as for the corridors, it is my belief they are infinite. No one has ever traveled all the corridors. Good day."

Stephen stood back, listening, as they flip-flopped out of sound.

"Can I be of help?" A barefooted monk grinned at him.

"I'm looking for the lady who lives off one of the corridors."

"I thought you might be. The door is there." The grinning monk pointed a worn finger to the stone wall.

"I see it now. Thank you."

Stephen knocked.

"Come in."

The room was packed tight with silence. The topology of wall, floor, and furniture were preglacial. The only hint of erosion was black and white latticework shutters.

The lady sat on the smooth marble sill of a window, her back to Stephen, her legs crossed, her eyes skimming the heads of the sheep to the sea.

"Viva, Stephen. Come sit awhile."

They sat, delighting their eyes in the relics of the meadow and the sea.

*

A week later, Stephen returned with the driftwood in a brown paper bag.

"I've come to show you the driftwood."

The lady held the driftwood pieces together, studying them quietly with her fingers and thumbs. Her gaze was fixed far out to sea.

Stephen waited.

Turning to Stephen, she fixed her gaze into his eyes and said, "For you,

Stephen and the driftwood, there are only two alternatives. The first one is to take the driftwood to the workshop here in the structure. Heat a small, pointed poker until it is red hot, then burn in the eyes quickly and gently. When the sockets cool, fill them with liquid wood made from the sawdust of the workshop. Once the liquid wood dries, sand it well so that it blends with the grain."

Then turning to the sea, the lady entered a river-like stillness…Stephen waited…

And waited…

Quietly, out of the stillness, she said, "The second choice you must discover."

*

Stephen returned to the corridor and his room off a corridor.

Up to this time, Stephen usually kept the driftwood in the brown paper bag on the top shelf of his clothes closet. He now removed the pieces from the bag, placing them on a small table where he observed them observing him.

*

A few weeks later, Stephen again visited the lady. He had hardly made himself comfortable next to her on the windowsill when she turned to him smiling. "Would you please read to me, Stephen?"

"Yes, of course."

She handed him a small brown book. The cover was threadbare and the binding loose. Many of the yellow pages were tea-stained. He opened at the bookmark and read.

"In the winters, I sometimes walk the corridors. One winter, in a corridor, I found an old key behind a broken clock. Holding it tightly, I went upstairs to look for a room. I found one. Tacked to the door was a neatly printed sign: **Please Do Not Enter.**

"I tried the key. It worked. I went in and opened wide the heavy velvet drapes. I was delighted. It was the old embroidery room, not used for years.

"Through a small hole in the windowpane, numerous swallows had entered the room and made nests. There were bits of clay, dried flowers, and straw scattered over the floor and furniture, the remnants of broken and discarded nests. The swallows, paying me no attention, sat still in new nests made from scraps of material, bits of lace, and threads of many colors. The nests were carefully placed on the chairs, love couch, and the two sewing tables.

"Looking around, I observed that most of the floor was free. So I returned

43

with my sewing things and a cushion, establishing myself on the floor. Not one swallow made a gesture toward me.

"The weeks passed, and I sewed and sewed. One day I brought in an orchid plant and gave it a space on the floor near me. It was a happy, healthy plant. The swallows took no notice.

"That winter was particularly cold, and my hands were often cramped from the drafts. At times I could barely thread a needle. Finally, with fear and reluctance, I decided to repair the window. I secured a pane of glass and puttied it in.

"When I returned the next day, the swallows were moving a little in their nests. Encouraged, I removed the cobwebs and lit a fire in the grate.

"About an hour later, a young swallow flew down from the sewing table and borrowed a piece of blue thread."

"Thank you, Stephen," the lady said.

"You're welcome," Stephen said and closed the book.

*

Nearly seven months passed. Stephen visited the lady every week. He was learning to listen … to wait. He read from St. John's Gospel. He observed the driftwood observing him.

One day he read this passage in John: "I am the Way, the Truth, and the Life." Stopping at the first four words—"I am the Way"—he repeated them slowly … often …

Near the end of February, Stephen decided to leave. There were a series of steps to be completed before the final act of leaving. These steps were completed by early April. Stephen decided to have a final visit with the lady.

*

Stephen and the lady sat on the windowsill. Suddenly a lamb sprang through the flock, chasing a cloud shadow. On the lamb went, gamboling near the edge. Suddenly it plunged over the cliff. The mother rushed about, filling the indifferent meadow with plaintiff calls.

The lady leaned to the warm noon. Then, lifting her hair, she tucked her soul beneath her hat.

"It's because of the fall," she said, "and the magician's death. But that is now all echoes eyes ago." Smiling to herself, she asked, "Does God have spies? Maybe so! Maybe so!"

"I am leaving today," Stephen said.

"Well, now … Would you like a cup of tea?"

"Yes, I'd love one."

The lady served the tea on a round, wrought-iron table with a glass top. They both sat and sipped away, enjoying the flavor and warmth.

"Oh my!" the lady said suddenly, "I nearly forgot. I have fresh-baked gingersnaps! Would you like some with your tea?"

"Yes, please," said Stephen, and smiling, added, "I have not had a fresh-baked gingersnap since I left home more than twelve years ago."

The lady fetched a plate of gingersnaps and placed it between them. More tea was poured, and they ate, dipping the gingersnaps in the tea.

Nine

Leaving the sprawling structure through the west wall, Stephen went down to the sea. He borrowed a rowboat.

Taking the driftwood, he rowed out about a mile.

Setting the driftwood pieces side by side on the crest of a wave, he waited …

Watching them drifting away, receiving together … c r e s t i n g … t r o u g h i n g …

The Marvelous Labyrinth of Love

One

Stephen went up to the city. He would travel and study. But first, he would study.

He found a room and went out into the street. It was a long, straight street. He walked slowly, his mouth slightly open, his mind musing, shaping.

The city is lean, he mused. *Lean and steep. Full of edges. And glass. Steep, steep, lean edges and walls of glass. Laser walls of clean, curtained glass.*

Even the horizontals are lean. No chopping. No clumsy crossing. No haphazard cross-purpose. Intersection. Neat, deliberate intersection.

The city is mind. Not matter and memory. Solitude. Desert. A vertical desert of fear and joy and a thousand pyramids standing neatly near each other's edges.

I love it, he mused, and went into a supermarket. He followed row after neat row, purchased, and appeared again in the street. All without speaking a word or losing his muse. *Survival is perfunctory*, he mused in his mind.

Smiling, he closed his mouth, nicely crossed an intersection, rounded a corner, and went down a straight, clean street to his room.

*

One day in summer, Stephen met Barbara. Soon they were together every day. Going here and there, doing things together. Delighting in hot summer days and warm evenings.

They were out into the country by now. On a dirt road, where dust lay thick on wild grasses in the ditches.

Climbing a slope to the crest of a hill, they sat down to lunch.

"Looks like rain clouds. What do you think?" said Stephen.

"I am rooted to where I am," replied Barbara.

"Good!" said Stephen. "We'll hide out here in the tall grass, and maybe the rain will miss us."

An hour later, they felt the rain bounce gently off their bodies.

It was dark when they arrived at Stephen's apartment. Barbara was quiet.

"I think I'll go straight home," she said.

"I thought you would stay the night!"

"Not tonight, Stephen. I just want to be alone."

An empty silence.

"Please, Stephen. I so want to be alone. You come by tomorrow."

"All right. But let me see you home."

"No, please. It's not far, and I'll be fine."

And kissing him quickly, she left.

51

That night Stephen had a strange dream.

He saw Barbara's form ahead of him on the pavement. She was walking quickly, unaware of his presence hurrying after her.

Suddenly she turned down an alley and began to run. Stephen followed.

On she ran, at an even distance from him. Repeatedly Stephen tried to increase his pace but could not. The alley had absorbed him, and he ran with its rhythm.

Moving his head back and forth, he squinted toward the distance but could see no end to the alley. He ran on, alone, naked and afraid. He had lost sight of Barbara ...

Now he could see her again, but only glimpses of her naked form, the curve of her, the quick, even movement of her long legs, her black hair making the darkness seem half light ...

Suddenly she stumbled into a blinding light. He stumbled too behind her, blinded by the light. When he opened his eyes, he had to shield them from the dense white light.

He could see now that Barbara had unwittingly run into a tree. She sat up and turned half toward him. Blood ran from a cut on her forehead and from her nose; it flowed into her eyes and mouth and dripped from her chin onto her breasts. She turned from him and threw her arms around the trunk of the tree.

The tree was dead, but it stood tall and stately as if it were alive; there was a readiness about it. Completely stripped of bark, its weathered, white wood was tender to the touch. The trunk-like body seemed to respond to Barbara's embrace, with its branch arms pointing here and there in the light.

Stephen knew instinctively he could not go to Barbara and she could not come to him. He was where he was. She was who she was. This was the given of the scene. What united him to her was the desire to know who she was; what drew her to him was the desire to find him.

Barbara let her blood drip and soak into the absorbent white wood. Then all of a sudden, the tree was gone and with it the light. Barbara stood up and walked over to a door and knocked.

A man appeared and said, "Yes, yes, what is it?"

"I'd like to wash my face."

"This is no time for jokes," replied the man impatiently. "There's a war on. There are wounded. Damn it, we need all the help we can get."

The man paused mechanically as if waiting for a response, then continued, "We have to patch the wounded and keep them moving. Damn it, there's a war on," he repeated, trying to convince himself of his own reality.

Without a word, Barbara disappeared through the doorway.

No sooner had she gone than the tree and the light reappeared, with Barbara sitting by the trunk, rocking back and forth with her arms around herself, crying.

Stephen felt cut off, out of touch. He envied the tree with its ability to absorb Barbara's blood through its skin and to stand there dead with life buried within.

Then Barbara stood up. The tree, the light were gone. She set off running down the alley.

Stephen followed.

Two

A few years passed. Stephen and Barbara were now married and lived first in the city and then in the country. They were happy together. Their life had a freedom and clarity.

"I'm free when I am with you," said Stephen.

"Free!" replied Barbara with her green eyes.

"When I was a boy," Stephen went on, "it would often thaw in March and then freeze. You could skate for miles on the glassy, open bay. I felt miles of space outside and inside."

*

They enjoyed the winter, cooking steaks in the fireplace on the hibachi. In the afternoon they were in the park with their children.

It was so cold they jumped up and down and ran to keep warm. Their breath puffed out white and thick, circling their faces a long time. When Barbara kissed Stephen's cheek, her lips were warm ice.

The children didn't want to go home.

"It's cold," Barbara explained. "Your father and I have had enough!"

"Just one more time walking on the brick wall," cried the children.

"Just one more!"

They had another turn.

"Just one more," they cried.

"No! We're leaving!"

Barbara and Stephen ran away. The children ran after them, crying and shouting.

"There! That's the end of that lot," said Barbara, coming down the carpeted stairs, listening with one ear for sound from above, smiling at the sudden quiet.

Soon they were eating steaks, drinking wine, sitting together on a leather couch near the coffee table.

"That was delicious," said Barbara, holding the wine glass to her lips. She was full and flushed. She felt her soul bubble up into her eyes.

Stephen, sitting at the other end of the couch, watched her through the clear, red gleam of his glass.

"What do you see, my love?" asked Barbara lazily.

"See?"

"Yes. See! What do you see through the clear, red gleam of your wine glass?"

"I see a great and wondrous happening."

"Tell me."

"I see the raisin of this world dried out and ready to be eaten by the starmaker."

"And what else?"

"I see the great goddess Barbara breaking out of this dried raisin and running smack toward the arms of the sun.

"But wait! Before she meets his arms, the starmaker rushes between them. In the midst of his rushing, he takes from his pocket a magnifying glass and holds it between the sun and Barbara. Before anyone can do anything, the starmaker burns a hole straight through Barbara's middle.

"The sun immediately takes his revenge and eats the starmaker. He turns then with fiery sad eyes to Barbara.

"But Barbara is not sad. She has just been born. She points proudly to the burned, black hole in her middle.

"However, it is all too much for the sun. So he reaches up into the sky and plucks a passing button. Gently he places the button in the hole in her belly. And now, he smiles. And that is how Barbara got her bellybutton."

"I like that story... But what were you doing?" asked Barbara, half seriously.

"Me? I was hanging for my life on the only grip left in the universe, the bottom grip of the quarter moon."

They laughed and talked a long time into their wine glasses and along the black, leather couch. Then they went up the carpeted stairs to bed and fell asleep quickly, with the wine throwing strings of stars and spirals before their eyes and through their blood.

The sun burned a hole straight through Stephen's forehead...

It was early morning.

They partially woke up.

Wholly made love.

A blend of dream and coincidence, a feeling of soft, green seaweed clinging to bare feet ... a momentary fright ... a springing from the bottom into the silky water of the pond.

They clung to each other,

The seaweed in their hair,

Drifting back to sleep.

As they drifted, Stephen saw them like parcels in a dark cupboard. They were packed or had packed themselves neatly near each other's wrappings. Their strings and ribbons touched, and their scotch-taped shoulders rubbed gently

in the cupboard

of

their

life.

Three

The nineteen eighties and the early nineties were full and intense.

Stephen continued to study, take notes, and search, but it was all done in snatches.

At the end we preferred to travel all night,
Sleeping in snatches,
With the voices singing in our ears, saying
That this is all folly.[4]

Stephen needed long periods of inner and outer silence to find an open field.

This became possible after 1995.

Comments on Question

In 1987 Barbara and I purchased a property in the country near Guelph, Ontario. It is a 12.8-acre field with a pond at the front and creek at the back. In the spring when the ice melts, the geese, ducks, and blue herons return to the creek to feed and to raise their young. Our home is in the middle of the field, making our driveway some three hundred meters long. Over the years, Barbara and I have used the driveway for our walk. If you walk the driveway up to the road and back to the garage, you have walked six hundred meters; if you do this ten times, you have walked six kilometers. We find the walk gives us the time and space not just for exercise, but also to unravel and to clarify the thousand and one knots flowing from our work, raising our three children, and the meaning of our day-to-day living.

Much of the imagery in the second answer to the question "Do I believe in God?" is taken from the various experiences of living in this beautiful field. One day I was standing at the back of the house looking down at the creek. Suddenly I sensed a presence near my right ear. I moved my head slowly to the right, and there was a diaphanous green hummingbird stopped in space staring at me. The fireplace mentioned in the same section is a wall made of field stones separating the family room from the living room. The wood fire, like the walking, has been essential in helping me to learn to listen and to muse quietly over what I was writing.

*

Question and Dialogue were written, for the most part, between 1994 and 2005. In the early nineties, a question, the same question, would often come to my mind, and I would turn it over and over. It would appear spontaneously when I was walking our long driveway, or when I was sitting musing, watching the dancing white and yellow flames of the wood fire. In one sense, it was a simple question because it is usually answered by an abstract definition given by the culture or group to which one belongs. In 1994, I turned sixty. By then I had spent twenty-eight years of my life searching for the meaning of the "there" I created by leaving Christianity and all organized religion. I was searching for "my" identity, not "an" identity, in the sense of being a member of a named group. The only group I could think of had the name "human." The question that I have been turning over and over since 1994 is: "What does it mean *for me* to be human?"

This question is very complex, for it involves all of what we name as reality. It involves in the beginning, before the beginning, nature, and a universe happening. It involves open, free, and trusting confrontation with words like: *God, religion, matter, spirit/mind,* and *birth/death.* It involves free and open connection with the profound mystery consciousness/the unconscious/ happening—which may be briefly expressed as: the lost, the forgotten, the unknown, and the treasure hard to attain. In a special way, it involves the word "where," for it is so easy to get lost in a world of words. We all know, at least implicitly, that the word, the sign, is not the reality. *Where* in space and time is the reality we seek with the word, the sign? I feel the answer to this question is intimately connected with the question "What does it *mean for me* to be human?"

Question—
A Primal Form of Search

Question!

To	ask	a	question	
Is	to	start	a	search.
To	start	a	search	
Is	to	be	human.	
To	be	human		
Is	a	question.		

Before the Beginning,
Or
Where Is God?

A Question

"Before the beginning" there appears to be "no matter," for in the beginning is the where/when of things beginning to matter. The immediate effect of a thing beginning to matter is space/time. That is why it is called: In (space) the Beginning (time).

MATTER?

In its "center" matter is "energy" "happening."

ENERGY?

The "center" of the "happening" is free and "open"

And is "mirrored" in consciousness/the unconscious.

"Matter" in its sensuous presence appears to be:

Things-with-parts-magnitude-and-position-moving-changing.

To change, to move is to-be-not-all-there. To-be-not-all-there is to be somewhere between "here" and "there." "Here" is the present point of mattering.

Where is "*there*"?

This is a complex question.

It is a question touching …

It is a question touching "m a t t e r" at the point of its mysteriously free and open grounding …

It is a question touching "c o n s c i o u s n e s s/t h e u n c o n s c i o u s" at the point of its mysteriously free and open grounding …

It is a question touching the-manifesting-of-an-inherent-aspect-of a t h i n g m a t t e r i n g … present-in-the-silence-of-an-open-being …

It is a question touching an-inherent-aspect-of "c o n s c i o u s n e s s/ t h e u n c o n c s i o u s m a n i f e s t i n g … present-in-the-silence-of-an-open-being …

It is a question touching the p r e s e n c e of-two-open-beings i n the-silence-of-each-other …

It is a question touching a p r e s e n c e beyond-s i l e n c e-where … two… open-beings-in-the-s i l e n c e-of-each-other … are p r e s e n t-in … o n e-s t i l l n e s s …

It is a question touching a p r e s e n c e beyond s i l e n c e where … o n e i s o n e' s s t i l l n e s s …

It is always a question touching …

Two Further Questions

If then there was a "before the beginning" and "before the beginning" means:

"*no-things-mattering,*"

further questions arise:

1. Is there "within" the matter flowing from "in the beginning," a-connection-with "before the beginning"?

And ...

2. Can I, who am part-of "in the beginning," "travel-to" and "cross-over-into" "before the beginning"?

A Search for Answers

When the primary concepts "in the beginning" and "before the beginning" are searched and faced, numerous questions and answers arise. In reply to the two questions raised, I will briefly consider, within the context of my search, two answers.

The first answer to these questions is to eliminate the concept "in the beginning." "Matter" has always mattered and will go on mattering "forever." The wheel turns and turns; and if there is no "in the beginning," there is no "before the beginning," in the sense of "no" matter whatsoever.

Modern cosmology appears to hint at this answer, but it leaves the door ajar to a second answer. Let us read carefully the following introduction to the Big Bang Theory:

> In the beginning there was an explosion. Not an explosion like those familiar on earth, starting from a definite center and spreading out to engulf more and more of the circumambient air, but an explosion which occurred simultaneously everywhere, filling all space from the beginning, with every particle of matter rushing apart from every other particle.[5]

This passage is from Steven Weinberg's book *The First Three Minutes*. In several sentences, we are introduced to a universe beginning to matter ... the beginning of a time/space "simultaneously everywhere ..."

But ... "what exploded"?

Is "what exploded" a "source" that in itself does not "matter" but can "cause" mattering? If we answer yes to this question, we have a second answer. The second answer says that "before the beginning," there was a "source" that did not "matter." And this "non-mattering-source" had the breathtaking capacity to "create" *t h i n g s* that "mattered."

The Traditional Answer of Western Culture

Western culture answers questions about "before the beginning" and "in the beginning" in one sentence. It is the first sentence of the Bible: "In the Beginning God created heaven and earth."

"In (space) the beginning (time)" sprang from a single point. This God does not matter but has the capacity to create *t h i n g s* that matter. This God then is not only the point of it all, heaven and earth, the entire universe; this God is the essential point *itself*: God is without parts and magnitude; but God, in the very act of creation, has position. There is an answer, within this answer, to the question "Where is God?"

Christianity took the concept of the Greek Logos (Plato, Aristotle, Plotinus) and boldly went to the crossover, an attempt at a crossing over with the Bible and reason into before the beginning. The major forays of this journey were made by the early church fathers and especially by St. Augustine. The culminating refinement is found in the writings of St. Thomas Aquinas.

St. Augustine, in his *Confessions*, describes in vivid, intense language his experience of the whereness of God. *The Confessions* of St. Augustine is one of the great dialogues of world literature. *The Confessions* is a series of dialogues involving Three: God, St. Augustine, and St. Augustine's unknown self. "I am," he writes, "a question to myself."

At the very beginning of these dialogues (Book 1, chapters 2 and 3), St. Augustine searches into the whereness of God:

2. And how shall I pray to my God, my God and my Lord? When I pray to Him, I call Him into myself... Can there be in me anything capable of containing you? Can heaven and earth contain you, heaven and earth which you made and in which you made me? Or, since nothing in existence could exist without you, does it therefore follow that everything that exists must contain you? I too exist. Why then do I ask you to enter into me? For unless you were in me, I could not exist. For after all I am not in Hell—and yet you are there too. For if I go down into Hell, Thou art there, I could not exist therefore, my God, were it not for your existence in me ...

3. You fill the heaven and the earth. Do they therefore contain you? Or after you have filled them, is there still something of you left over, since they are unable to contain you?... Shall we not rather say this: everywhere you are present in your entirety, and no single thing can contain you in your entirety?[6]

Whereness expresses a-connection-with. Here St. Augustine speaks of an ultimate metaphysical connection: "I could not exist therefore, my God, were it not for your existence in me." Christianity in its search for the whereness-of-God seeks over and over again for a more immediate, tangible connection.

The Search for the "Whereness-of-God"

The search for the "whereness-of-God" created within Western culture is a focus of unity and division. For the search for the "whereness-of-God" was a search for an *acceptable-tangible-connection-point* with God. It was a search springing from the question "Where specifically-here-and-now do I find ultimate truth and ultimate good?"

The concrete answers given and creating the unity and division within Western culture were:

1. In community
   (ecclesia)
2. In appointed authority
   of the community
3. In the direct revelation
   of word (the Bible)
4. In the free and open grounding
   of human consciousness

Whether or not this question regarding "ultimate truth" and "ultimate good" may be, in its wording, fundamentally misleading is another question. For me, however, in my search, the consideration of whereness is fundamental. The questioning into *where* in all its primary meanings:

Where am I?
Where did I come from?
Where am I going?
is a questioning into a central aspect of the mystery of the grounding of "matter," the grounding of "consciousness/unconsciousness," which I call a search for "there."

Thomas Aquinas and the Whereness-of-God

Thomas Aquinas took the metaphysics of the Greek Logos, as found in Aristotle, and built a kind of ladder—a ladder reaching into the source of all being, the very point of "before the beginning."

The metaphysics of Aristotle is grounded in certain conceptual pairs: matter and form, act and potency, substance and accident, essence and existence. Thomas took these concepts and created a metaphysics based on *existence* and expressed through a difficult, strange, and flexible concept called analogy. Not the analogy of the common metaphor, where one thing is in some way like another. Thomas employs an analogy of proper proportionality, where what is said (or predicated) is said to mean: "every being exercises: the act of existence (is) in proportion to its essence."[7]

Thomas begins by saying: every real being has essence and existence. The essence is *what-a-thing-is* (a noun); the existence is *that-it-is*, the cause of, the act that is the *to-be* of a thing (a verb). Essence determines the limit of the existence of a being. So Thomas would proceed saying, "A rock, in its essence of rockness, *is* more limited than a tree. A tree, in its essence of treeness, *is* more limited than a dog. A dog, in its essence of dogness, *is* more limited than a human. A human, in its essence of humanness, *is* more limited than an angel."

Now, God's essence is *to be (existence)*. God is pure act. In God, essence and existence are *one*! God is not a noun; God is a verb! Not just in a "grammatical" sense but in a real sense. As pure act, God has no limits. And primarily God does not matter. "Matter" in the sense of a substance … to move/to change, to be *not-all-there*. God is fully and perfectly *there*. And I am *here*!

Has Thomas, with reason and the Bible, really travelled from "here" to "there"? In his unfinished *Summa Theologica,* he writes:

> When the existence of a thing has been ascertained there remains the further question of the manner of its existence, in order that we know its essence.

Now because we cannot know what God is, but rather what He is not, we have no means for considering how God is, but rather how He is not.[8]
And again:

> This is the extreme of human knowledge of God: to know that we do not know God.[9]

There is also an answer found in a saying attributed to Thomas in the last year of his life. He died at the age of forty-nine in 1274. It is this saying, even more than what he wrote, that binds me to his memory. Thomas had a vivid inner experience, a mystical experience; and after this experience, he refused to return to his writing. When urged to complete his *Summa*, he replied:

"I cannot write anything further. In the light of what I have experienced, I now perceive all that I have written as straw."

Other Connections with "Before the Beginning"

There are, however, besides reason, other connections with "before the beginning." One central to Western culture is faith, or belief.

My search for the *t h e r e* began as a search for an open field where I might discover the answer to "Who am I?" And the search for an open field led me to search for a point that would give me a stand where I might discover the answer to "Where am I?" It gave me a leaving point, a leaving point that is both a leaving and a taking-with.

The leaving is the leaving of the structure—the corridors, the rooms, the stairs leading to more corridors and rooms—all of which, in turn, lead to a forgetfulness to create doors-outward where there are endless open fields.

The taking-with is the search to-be-one-with an inner vision that is manifested variously and repeatedly within this strange and manifold Western culture. And intimately connected with this inner vision of Western culture is a powerful, varying, tenuous presence expressed in a deceitfully naive and apparently simple word: *God*!

A favorite question of Western culture is to ask oneself:

"Do I believe in God?"

Twice over the years since I left the priesthood, Christianity, and all organized religion, I have attempted to answer this question in writing.

Do I Believe in God?
(First Answer, circa 1977)

When I was a child, I climbed trees. I loved to climb trees. Deciduous trees were my favorite climb, although I did climb many an evergreen and I can still sense the distinct texture and aroma of the fir, spruce, and pine that grew in the endless miles of woods near our home.

I do believe that tree climbing has almost disappeared as a form of childhood adventure. This to me is sad. The two elements essential to my formation in childhood were climbing trees and hiking in the woods. These adventures spring spontaneously from being a child. To climb a tree and to hike in the woods are to pass beyond questions. In these two acts of instinctive adventure, the child is question and answer in one. And such a child in later life is perfectly at home with Ludwig Wittgenstein when he says that a philosophical problem has the form: "I don't know my way about." And with Martin Heidegger, who is constantly asking questions and is not afraid to admit that questions frequently lead one *"auf dem Holzwege"* (on the woodcutter's path).

Many of us spend our entire lives *"auf dem Holzwege."* This in itself is not the tragedy. The tragedy lies in never being aware that one is *"auf dem Holzwege."* This saying, *"auf dem Holzwege,"* on the woodcutter's path, is similar to the French *"cul de sac,"* blind alley. However, I find the German expression a more vivid image of human experience. The path made by the woodcutter will eventually end. It does not lead home. It was made only to find and cut wood. It ends suddenly and leads into the dense uncharted woods. If we continue, we may well be lost in the woods.

We can all sense the horror of being lost in the woods. When I was a child, they would blow the mill whistle when someone was reported lost in the woods. And a wave of fear would spread through the town.

One of the great searches in Western literature starts as follows:

HALFWAY ALONG THE JOURNEY of our life,
Having strayed from the right path and lost it,
I awoke to find myself in a dark wood.

Dante, in *The Divine Comedy*, is beginning his search into the *q u e s t i o n* *"Where is love?"*

*

Every genuine question begins somewhere in a dark wood, for it springs from the anguish of being lost. As Dante says:

> O how hard it is to tell what it was like
> That wild and mighty and unfriendly forest,
> The very thought of which renews my fear!
> So bitter was it that death could be no worse.

But Dante continued. He walked on, continued his search, and in the midst of his terror found his guide. He says:

> But, to reveal what benefit it brought me,
> I shall tell of the other things I found.[10]

The question "Do I Believe in God?" is for me, where I now stand, not a genuine question. It is not my question! It is a question springing from the sound of words, not the stillness of my center.

Do I Believe in God?
(Second Answer, circa 1994)

To begin, I can only say, using a colloquial phrase, "I would to God I understood the question!" When I say "understood" or "understand" the question, I am saying that I do not stand under, I am not rooted in, the meaning toward which these symbols point. What do I really know when somebody asks me this question, or when I ask myself this question? Where do I find a standing *point* to *understand* in the midst of the ambiguity arising from the *sound* and *fury* of countless groups and countless centuries shouting countless meanings for this one symbol?

I write the question with my black ballpoint on a sheet of ruled, white paper: **Do I believe in God?**

I stand before the question and strip myself completely naked in my body and my mind—completely naked in my imagination, my emotions, my entire being. I then take the question and place it in my naked mind's eye; and going forth naked in my body, I travel with the question. I climb with the question to the uttermost peak of the highest mountain. I stand with it naked on the peak, and oblivious to the cold, I look through the question into the very eye of the sun and the moon. I stand there almost forever. And the question is always before me; I am never under the question. Look as I may, I cannot reach out and touch and taste the roots of these symbols. And when I turn away naked and frozen, the question is still standing just before my mind's eye, each word frozen individually.

I am now again on the flat, warm earth. It is summer. I stand in the middle of a huge, rolling hay field. The soft fragrance of clover and alfalfa blends with the perfume of the wildflowers. Bobolinks perching on the hay stalks swoop in the air eating invisible insects. Thousands of white and brown butterflies are quietly busy before the faces of the flowers.

I sit down naked in the middle of the living field and prop up the question anew: **Do I believe in God?**

Each word has now thawed, and the whole sentence hangs loosely together in the summer sun. Suddenly the word God and the question mark are blurred by the presence of a diaphanous green hummingbird standing still near my right ear. It stands perfectly still, a green flame the size of my thumb; only the transparent, infinite wings move. Its beauty is pure silence. The bobolinks and the butterflies do not know that I am naked, but the hummingbird knows. Have you ever seen a hummingbird smile? Just the trace of movement near its beak. It's breathtaking!

I sit in the middle of the hay field all summer. The bobolinks are busy every day perching gently on the hay stalks and swooping to eat invisible insects. The butterflies quietly move day after day like music before the flowers. The hummingbird appears every day, stands still near my right ear, and smiles, just the trace of a movement near its beak.

At the end of the summer, I get up from the middle of the hay field and go home. I put on underwear, jogging pants, and a loose warm sweater. After a search, I find my blue canvas shoes in the family room near the bookshelves. I am hungry and thirsty. I cook a hot meal of sauce and pasta and open a bottle of red wine.

It is late September and cool enough to light a fire in the fireplace. As I sit before the warm wood fire, I suddenly realize what has happened. As I was searching for my blue canvas shoes, the question "Do I believe in God?" slipped from my mind's eye and fell down by the chair near the window. I am now comfortable and tired. But I am also driven. Driven by the matter, or the missing of a matter in the question. So I search out the question and find it by the chair near the window.

I return to the couch and the fire and prop up the question once again in my mind's eye. I look through each word into the soft, white-yellow flame of the fire. I wait... At some point in the waiting, I sense the missing matter.

There is *no s i l e n c e* in the grouping of these words.

Now I Return to Ask

Now I return to ask: "What is this intimate connection between the inner vision, manifested variously and repeatedly within Western culture, and a powerful, varying, tenuous presence called 'God'?"

Tentatively the connection may be called "the *waiting*"!

The waiting is a form of leaving, the leaving of being left behind in one's stillness.

The waiting springs from and creates a soft whisper … any whisper, … such as:

En una noche oscura (On a very dark night)[11]

or …

Ein Hauch um nichts (A breath about nothing)[12]

or …

The waiting

Is the waiting

Of the dark-sided moon,

The waiting of a child's spoon,

The murmur of lost in the wood,

The grave digger so little understood,

and

sitting

by the tree

in

s t i l l n e s s.

Comments on Dialogue

I began to write the final part, "Dialogue," in 1994. Each of the parts was first written by hand in a hard-covered notebook. Before I began to write these comments, I read through the notebook. In the first ten pages, I attempted three times to answer the question "Where does dialogue begin?"

One of the answers was: "Dialogue begins in discovery of a silence within the self, a silence imbued with four furrows:

    The lost
    The forgotten
    The unknown
    The treasure hard to attain

The furrows are the soft sand of nature, the nakedness of the self, creating an open field where I might search for a concealed word.

As I began writing "Dialogue," I sensed and knew I had found a field, a field giving me a stand somewhere outside Western culture. It is a meadow of wildflowers and grasses, growing in a loose, sandy soil.

My search into:

    In the beginning
    Before The beginning
    Nature
    led me to this field.

The "Dialogue" seeks to clarify, to confirm my stand within the field. The "Dialogue" is a search into the expression of nature and the four furrows in Western culture and the found field.

Dialogue—
A Primal Form of Search

Dialogue!

the dialogue
is the dialogue
in an open field,
spoken without reservation,
grounded in the silence of
the-i-and-the-i
and
the-searched-concealed-word.

Nature
and
the Four Furrows
in
Western Culture

The Parameters of Searching
These Concealed-Words
Within Western Culture

I am in the found field. I am attempting to enter into a Dialogue with Western culture. The dialogue is a searching into "meaning," into an "experiencing" of certain concealed-words.

The words:

Nature

The lost

The forgotten

The unknown

The treasure hard to attain are historically concealed in the "records" of the culture, in writings, material remains, art forms, and so on. But "records" are not the "experiencing" of the concealed-words. At all material times, the words arose-from and were nourished-within an "individual consciousness."

Each "individual consciousness" is a "contained" field. It is "contained" because consciousness in its forms and manifestation only exists in "an individual." In order for an individual consciousness to be part of a culture it must "experience" and accept certain fundamental "meanings" arising-from and maintained-within the culture. These "meanings," taken together, form "a world."

A fundamental tendency of consciousness is to seek and establish a specific form of orientation within "a world." This tendency may be called "a search into whereness."

Where am I?

Where did I come from?

Where am I going?

The "I" is the conscious "individual ego." This dialogue is grounded in "the silence of the 'i' and the 'i.'" The 'i' is the "self." The "self" is not immediately present within the context of consciousness. The "self" is a symbol of the "capacity" within each individual to be "whole," to be fully *there*!

The "wholeness" arises from a continuous-connecting-as-one-of an individual consciousness with its unconscious and "a world."

If, however, "a world" (a given culture) tends to exteriorize individual consciousness, then dialogue, as expressed above, becomes remote in proportion to the extent of the exteriorization. I speak here of the "open field" and the silence of each 'i'. With this in mind, I tentatively proceed to the search of the concealed-words.

Where Is Nature in the Experience of Western Culture?

I begin with the concealed-word nature. Nature in the experience of Western culture appears to reveal itself as *out-there*.

The roots of this experiencing of nature as *out-there* may be found largely within written records and archeological research. The records and research reveal various sources shaping the experiencing of nature as *out-there*.

A Primary Source

About four thousand years ago, a nomadic tribe in the Middle East began, very slowly, to have an experience of a "unique" god. The "unique" was the living breath of their experience. For this god was not just another tribal god (each tribe had their own god); this god was the *one God* above all gods.

The main outlines of the development of this experiencing were written in Hebrew in five books, between 900 and 700 B.C., and were called the Torah.

The first book, Genesis, sets out where the tribe came from and where all of nature and all humans came from. Everything that exists came from the *one God* through an act of creation.

Now, when God finished creating heaven and earth and all creatures, including the first man and the first woman, God looked at it all and said: "This is very good!" The word "good" meant that all of creation, in the finished act, was fully and completely *there*. "Good" had no opposite. The entire "world" was a paradise. There was no morality in the sense of good and bad human acts. There were no physical privations, such as hunger and disease.

Then a very strange event occurred. It happened that God placed two fruit-bearing trees in the middle of paradise. One was the tree of life, and the other was the tree of the knowledge of good and evil.

God loved what he created so much that he would, in the cool of an afternoon, walk in the midst of paradise and speak to the humans, Adam and Eve. And as he spoke, they sensed how much he loved every aspect of creation, and especially them, created in his own image.

On one of these walks, God said to the humans that they may eat the fruit of any tree in paradise, except the fruit of the tree of the knowledge of good and evil.

Then it happened that one day they did eat the fruit of the tree of the knowledge of good and evil. God walking in the garden discovered their act and became angry and punished them. He placed sanctions on them, he made them clothes because they had become acutely aware that they were naked, and then he sent them forth from the garden.

But the very heart of the punishment was this: God withdrew his presence from paradise, from the whole created world. He no longer visited them nor walked with them nor talked to them. God went away, high into the heavens. He became the *God-out-there*, who only spoke to them through messengers (angels), signs, and a few chosen humans. And nature itself without the presence of God became obscure and unknown. It became strange, unpredictable, hostile, and threatening.

Nature became *out-there*, the human body became *out-there*, and the inner-roots that fed the spirit became *out-there*.

This account in the first three chapters of Genesis is usually called "the creation and the fall." It is important to note that there are two separate accounts of creation, and of the creation of humans. The fall is found in the second account.

The fall is indeed "strange." The strangeness arises from the presence of an underlying content and meaning. On the surface, the fall appears as the individual "acts" of two humans deciding and then doing something, acts of disobedience. However, this is not what God was upset about.

The text reads:

> Yahweh God made tunics of skins for the man and his wife and clothed them. Then Yahweh God said, "Now that the man has become like one of us in knowing good from evil, he must not be allowed to reach out his hand and pick from the tree of life too, and eat and live for ever!" So Yahweh God expelled him from the garden of Eden, and so on, and put guards at the gate.[13]

The text speaks of a knowledge of nakedness and knowing good from evil.

They knew good before they ate the fruit. What they knew after they ate the fruit was "nakedness" and "good in relation to evil." The "evil" was not moral evil. Nor was the nakedness "physical nakedness." Knowing good/evil together made them "one of us"—divine!

The "fall" is about knowledge, an experiencing knowledge of a self-reflective human consciousness. It is the knowledge arising from the "in-there" of an individual consciousness connecting with out-there, symbolized in the reaching out of the hand, the taking of the fruit, and the eating of the fruit. What they discovered as "nakedness" was a glimpse into the mystery of the "unknown within."

As I was reflecting on the first three chapters of Genesis, I came across a book by Robert Graves and Raphael Patai called *Hebrew Myths—The Book of Genesis*. On the nakedness of Adam and Eve, they quote from an aprocryphal Book of Adam, preserved in an Armenian text and translated into German by Erwin Preuschen in 1900:

> Adam wondered at Eve's nakedness: because her glorious outer skin, a sheet of light smooth as a finger-nail, had fallen away. Yet though the beauty of her inner body, shining like a white pearl, entranced him, he fought for three hours against the temptation to eat and become as she was; holding the fruit in his hand meanwhile. At last he said: "Eve, I would rather die than outlive you. If Death were to claim your spirit, God could never console me with another woman equalling your loveliness!" So saying, he tasted the fruit, and the outer skin of light fell away from him also.[14]

Sources Influencing the Primary Source

The above account relating the beginning and fall of nature passed through mainstream Judaism to a sect of Judaism, which eventually broke from Judaism and became known as Christianity. Christianity accepted the Torah and other Jewish Scriptures as the revealed word of the *one God*.

The early growth of Christianity was influenced and subtly colored by other sources. One of these was ancient Greek culture, in its Classical and Hellenistic forms. The New Testament was written in the Koine Greek of the Hellenistic Period.

Now I Turn To The Four Furrows In Western Culture

From where I stand in the found field, I see the four furrows in Western culture as a profound awareness of human consciousness be*ing ** in-matter.

It is a perspective gleaned and cultivated by repeated sojourns into the account of the creation and the fall, and into the transcendent and the abstract. It is the perspective of:

> *One* who is *above,*
> Higher-than, better-than,
> More-pure-and-perfect-than ...
> And
> this perceiving/experiencing
> *"P a r t"*
> is called:
> psyche ... pneuma
> soul ... spirit
> And
> what is perceived
> Below or over-against-it
> is called:
> hyle ... soma
> matter ... body

This perspective, creating two distinct worlds, a material world and a spiritual world, forms a central dynamic in the growth of Western culture. It appeared in Plato's philosophy and produced a remarkable revolution in Greek thought. Greek scholars have repeatedly searched into this revolution and its meaning for Western culture. Here is a quote from E. R. Dodds's book *The Greeks and the Irrational*, which is based on a series of lectures that he gave at Berkeley in the autumn of 1949:

> Whether it be true or not that on the lips of an ordinary fifth-century Athenian the word psyche had or might have a faint flavour of the uncanny, what it did not have was any flavour of Puritanism or any suggestion of metaphysical status. The "soul" was no reluctant prisoner of the body, it was here that the new religious pattern made its fateful contribution: by crediting man with an occult self of divine origin, and thus setting soul and body at odds, it introduced

into European culture a new interpretation of human existence, the interpretation we call puritanical.[15]

In the early centuries A.D., dualism was a major element in the development of religious and philosophical thought. There was the dualism of Plato, Gnosticism, Manichaeism, and other Middle East and Far Eastern influences. The morality flowing from dualism tends to be puritanical in its attitude toward matter and physical pleasures. In Western culture, it reached a peak with Calvin and his followers. According to R. H. Tawney:

> The most characteristic and influential form of Protestantism in the two centuries following the Reformation is that which descends, by one path or another, from the teaching of Calvin. Unlike the Lutheranism from which it sprang, Calvinism, assuming different shapes in different countries, became an international movement, which brought, not peace, but a sword, and the path of which was strewn with revolutions. Where Lutheranism had been socially conservative, deferential to established political authorities, the exponent of a personal, almost a quietistic, piety, Calvinism was an active and radical force. It was a creed which sought, not merely to purify the individual, but to reconstruct Church and State and to renew society by penetrating every department of life, public as well as private, with the influence of religion.[16]

Friedrich Heer points out:

> Calvinists were "the pioneers of the modern world." They developed the religious forces of Western Europe in the sixteenth century, its international politics in the seventeenth century, and its science in the eighteenth century. They created the new Europe of work, ambition, colonialism, war-economy and natural science. Through them, Europe first became wholly Western. They completed a development which had begun with the Roman popes, the Gregorian reforms and scholasticism. The inner history of Europe after the Calvinist period, that is, from the nineteenth century on, was an attempt to overcome the attitudes fixed by the Calvinists...
>
> Calvin had an eye for the political realities of his age and he knew where his doctrine had favourable prospects. The very essence of the doctrine was a kind of social theory. An inescapable division of mankind into two classes had been made at the time of creation. There were two nations, the elect and the damned. An unknowable

God, whose purposes were obscure, had ordained this division and man with all his works was helpless before it...

Calvin was the first to try to seize systematically the entire inner life of man. The "City of God" confiscated everything, including the individual's subconscious drives. Geneva was to be a model cell for a total world revolution. Thus Calvin carried Plato's expulsion of the poets and Aristotle's conception of the primacy of the communal over the individual to their logical conclusion.[17]

"Calvin was the first to try to seize systematically the entire inner life of man." This may well be so if one emphasizes the "seize systematically," but not if one says "to control the entire inner life." The early centuries in the growth of Christianity are a history of "heresy." Once Christianity became the official religion of the Roman Empire, it was made clear and enforced that the "inner-roots that fed the spirit" of the individual person were not to be trusted. All truth and all good comes from the out-there of the community, and specifically the interpretive authority of the community.

I will now continue the dialogue from the perspective of the found field.

Nature
and
the Four Furrows
in
the Found Field

Where Is Nature in the Experience of the Found Field?

Nature is *here and now!*... If I-as-one-reach-out-and-reach-in, nature is manifest. Nature is the sum of all *t h i n g s*. Nature is somet *h i n g*, anyt *h i n g*, *and* everyt *h i n g*.

Nature is also no-thing! It is no-thing that makes nature manifest. No-thing is the grounding and the point from which everything emerges. Nature is continually ex-isting out of no-thing. Nature manifests as the here and now. The essence of nature is the continual moving from a here and now to a there.

No-thing has been called by many names. It has been called Atman, Nirvana, God, Void, Primary Ground; in short, *it* has been called by a thousand and one names. Each time and times, when I stand up and *name* no-thing without parts and magnitude, no-thing vanishes, and I am left with the illusion of ... the *name*!

Yes, I know! I am naked, in the dark and alone, without a name! I am in silence! The living word, the name, emerges from silence as a somet *h i n g* emerges from no-thing. However, the *name* is not the *s i l e n c e*!

In the found field, no-thing has no name! For the name no-thing is a pure symbol ... p o i n t i n g ...

Certain Realities with an Affinity to No-Thing

Nothing:

Nothing manifests an affinity with no-thing in that it reveals a presence of no-thing. Nothing tends to take on a metaphysical edge when conceived in the abstract as an absolute. Nothing, however, is a *t h i n g*! It is vital in all our connections with things, the absence in things, and the absence of things.

The reality of nothing as a thing is best grasped by reflecting on several examples of the powerful active presence of nothing.

Nothing as a *t h i n g* is manifested in an abstract way in arithmetic by the symbol zero (0). Zero is one of the ten symbols used to express all numbers. Tobias Danzig, in his book *Number: The Language of Science*, begins his chapter on zero with a quote from Pierre Laplace:

> It is India that gave us the ingenious method of expressing all numbers by means of ten symbols, each symbol receiving a value of position as well as an absolute value; a profound and important idea which appears so simple to us now that we ignore its true merit. But its very simplicity and the great ease which it has lent to all computations put our arithmetic in the first rank of useful inventions; and we shall appreciate the grandeur of this achievement the more when we remember that it escaped the genius of Archimedes and Apollonius, two of the greatest men produced by antiquity.[18]

The Indian term for *zero* (*zero* is Italian) is *sunya,* which means empty or blank. Danzig ends the chapter on zero as follows:

> Conceived in all probability as the symbol for an empty column on a counting board, the Indian sunya was destined to become the turning-point in a development without which the progress of modern science, industry, or commerce is inconceivable... In the history of culture the discovery of zero will always stand out as one of the greatest single achievements of the human race.

*

Nothing as a *t h i n g* is manifested in a physical and mystical manner in chapter XI of the *Tao Te Ching* by Lao Tzu:

We put thirty spokes together and call it a wheel;

But it is on the space where there is nothing that the usefulness of the wheel depends.
We turn clay to make a vessel;
But it is on the space where there is nothing that the usefulness of the vessel depends.
We pierce doors and windows to make a house;
And it is on these spaces where there is nothing that the usefulness of the house depends.
Therefore just as we take advantage of what is, we should recognize the usefulness of what is not.[19]

*

Nothing as a *t h i n g* manifests itself as the spiritual capacity to experience the silence of meaning in the following Zen story:

A Cup of Tea
Nan-in, a Japanese master during the Meiji era (1868–1912), received a university professor who came to inquire about Zen.
Nan-in served tea. He poured his visitor's cup full, and then kept on pouring.
The professor watched the overflow until he no longer could restrain himself. "It is overfull. No more will go in!"
"Like this cup", Nan-in said, "you are full of your own opinions and speculations. How can I show you Zen unless you first empty your cup?"[20]

*

Nothing as a *t h i n g* manifests itself at the center of creative imagination. Consider this statement by Leonardo da Vinci:

Among the great things which are found among us the existence of Nothing is the greatest.[21]

*

Consciousness:
I begin to exist at the moment of becoming one cell. This "happening" is a gift of a unique half-mother and a unique half-father ... soon I begin to divide and grow ... making discoveries as I do so... then one day I am born into a world.

97

Tentatively, touchingly, I move within a flow ... a flow like a river. I come to the surface ... drift below the surface ... slowly ... very slowly ... I sense a "happening" in me ... coming to me from a center of two points joined ... inside/outside ... above the surface ... below the surface ... on and on... consciousness "happened" to me ... I did not will or produce consciousness... It awoke within me from the inward/outward ... above-the-surface/below-the-surface ... c o n n e c t i o n s ... like breathing!

The nature of consciousness eludes me, first of all, because consciousness is and is-not a thing! It may manifest within me as image, memory, idea ... or as experience, emotion ... and so on.... However, it eludes me most of all because consciousness is not-all-there!

Consciousness reveals itself as a living edge, a touching-presence of no-thing ...

This-touching-presence reveals itself in the form: consciousness craves connection ...

Consciousness primarily and innately craves connection with its own Be*xxx*ing.

Who am I?

Where am I?

What is my meaning?

Such questions speak from the roots of my Be*xxx*ing and are profoundly expressed in the perennial human awareness of:

The lost

The forgotten

The unknown

The treasure hard to attain

Answers are discoverable in a continuous, life-long-connection between consciousness and its roots ... the never-sleeping, continually creating, forming, nourishing presence called the unconscious.

*

The Unconscious:

The unconscious is to consciousness as the roots of a tree are to the trunk, branches, and foliage. A tree is inconceivable without its root system, which reaches down into the dark soil grounding and nourishing the trunk, branches, and foliage.

The root system exists in the dark and feeds in the darkness of the soil. The trunk, branches, and foliage exist in the light and feed on the light. The dark and the light sides of the tree intimately depend on one another. There is no growth without this dependent connection.

My experience, my knowledge, my formed words have to sink down into the roots of my darkness and feed there in silence, in stillness, in a process of waiting.

If this does not "happen" (and I must be open to the "*hap*" that is always *there*), then I will spend my *l i f e* with a head full of w o r d s, or even worse, a heart full of w o r d s that bounce off one another continually without meaningful connection ... connections that can only be found where the treasure is hidden ... in the living connection field of:

consciousness/the unconscious/and "a world happening."

*

"Hap":

The word "hap" is no longer in common use. It is the root of happen and happiness, and is found in Middle English and Old Norse. The underlying meaning is: some event occurs without apparent cause. Following this meaning, I cannot will or pursue happenings or happiness. They occur in a spontaneous connection of in-there and out-there. What I can do is wait and listen.

Epilogue

Leaving Western Culture

I left Western culture by discovering the found field. The center of the found field is freedom—a freedom creating a perspective, an openness to see from the "outside"; as seeing an "identifiable group" as one who is not part of that "group." It is not a perspective of alienation. It is a perspective of openness to every human being I meet.

It is a perspective flowing from the conviction that to be human cannot be defined in an abstract or definitive manner, for every human has the capacity to develop a unique transcending and transforming perspective.

The Search Continues

As I finish this essay, I am a month away from being seventy-six. The search continues! There is an "infinity" to discover in the found field.

The found field is my conscious/unconscious-connecting-with-"a world." This field may be described as a "singularity," defined by Michael Guillen as "a mathematical point at which some quantity is infinite." He ends his chapter on Natural Infinities/Singular Ideas as follows: "The oldest piece of evidence for a fully contained infinity is the mind itself. For, although infinity is confined in the mind within a volume that is relatively large compared to that of an electron or a black hole, the mind is no less singular than these."[22]

Jung writes from the perspective of psychology: "Theoretically, no limits can be set to the field of consciousness, since it is capable of indefinite extension. Empirically, however, it always finds its limit when it comes up against the unknown."[23]

He then describes the unknown as the outside experienced by the senses and the inside experienced immediately. The inner unknown is the unconscious.

The Partially Known

There are "hidden realities" and a "sensed presence" in certain words, the words I only partially know—words such as matter and spirit, briefly touched on above. In the perspective of the found field, the grounding of matter and spirit are one. I tentatively call this source no-thing.

There is also a strange mystery concealed in the words birth and death… The presence of a birth connects me with joy, love, awe, and celebrating… There is a spontaneous impulse to utter, "This is indeed wondrous strange!" This impulse appears to be a universal aspect of consciousness and may be summed up: "It is good to be born!" From the perspective of the found field, it follows: "Therefore, it is good to die!" However, in Western culture, the pair birth and death has been fused with morality.

Which brings me to two more words that are central to my continuous search. These words are breathing and morality. The primary connection a human makes on leaving the womb is the connection of breathing. Breathing is an inner/outer connection where the inner organs open and reach out to the outer air/oxygen. Another primary connection a human makes at a very early age is the connection with the mores, customs, and conventions regarded as vital to the social group.

The morality of the found field sees a profound analogy between the breathing that connects with the physical-time-space world and a morality that connects within a group-time-space world. The essence of the analogy is the immediate, ever-present connection between the inner/outer, both being a flow of receiving/giving. The growth of this morality springs from an immediate and ever-present connection with the buried point of the stillness of my center. I grow as an infant, child, and young person by learning and respecting the rules and customs of my immediate social world, and learning to break through in my thirties into a realized touching of my stillness. And in my late fifties into a touching knowledge, a knowledge that is not belief. This morality that is analogous with breathing does not in any way spring from a need of redemption, salvation, or reward. It arises from a continuous search for a knowledge that creates a transforming center.

*

When I say "knowledge," I mean "*c o n n e c t i o n*," "connection" that is a happening and an awareness—the connection of love, joy, and wonder. To come closer to the meaning of the "connection" I call "knowledge," I may ask myself: "Where am I when I am *i n - l o v e*?" The answers, in both sign and word, are many indeed, for they reflect the uniqueness of each individual consciousness. Shakespeare, in *The Tempest*, has Prospero say, observing his daughter Miranda and Ferdinand meeting: "At the first sight they have changed eyes."[24] I describe it as a thereness:... the p r e s e n c e of-two-open-beings ... i n the-silence-of-each-other ... present-i n o n e-s t i l l n e s s ...

The Unknown

Then there are the words God and religion. Every organized religion creates its own God or gods. In this context, the word religion is more fundamental than the word God. Religion points to an inherent aspect of human consciousness: the need to continuously discover meaningful connections with one's self and others in a universe "happening"!

The more I search into the meaning and significance of these words, the more I know that I can leave the words and the images created by organized religion, but not a presence I sense in the grounding of the words. It is a presence that transcends words, but it is as tangible and real as the presence I feel in being - *i n* - love with Barbara.

Notes

1. T. S. Eliot, *The Complete Poems and Plays—1909–1950* (New York: Harcourt, Brace & World, Inc., 1971) p. 234.

2. Mircea Eliade, *Myth and Reality* (New York: Harper & Row, Publishers Incorporated, 1963) p. 1.

3. Michel de Montaigne, *Essays, in Three Volumes*, Translated by John Florio, 1603 (London: Dent; New York: Dutton; London: Everyman's Library, 1965) Volume One, Chapter 22, p. 105.

4. T. S. Eliot, *The Complete Poems and Plays*, p. 68.

5. Steven Weinberg, *The First Three Minutes—Updated Edition* (Cambridge: Massachusetts Basic Books, A Division of Harper Collins Publishers, 1988) p. 5.

6. St. Augustine, *The Confessions*, Translated by Rex Warner (New York: A Mentor Book, Published by the Penguin Group, 1963) pp.18–19.

7. Gerald B. Phelan, *Saint Thomas and Analogy, The Aquinas Lecture*, 1941 (Milwaukee: Marquette University Press, 1943).

8. Thomas Aquinas, *Summa Theologica*, Part 1, q. 3, Translated by Anton C. Pegis (New York: The Modern Library—New York, Random House Inc., 1945, 1948) p. 28.

9. Josef Pieper, *Scholasticism*, quoting Thomas Aquinas, *Quaest. Disp. De Potentia Dei* Part 7, Question 5 ad14 (New York, Toronto: McGraw-Hill Book Company, Pantheon Books Inc. 1960) p. 54.

10. Dante, *The Divine Comedy—Inferno*, Translated into blank verse by Louis Biancoli (New York: Washington Square Press, 1966) p. 1.

11. St. John of the Cross, *The Poems of St. John of The Cross, The Spanish Text*, with a translation by Roy Campbell (Glasgow: Harvill Press Ltd., 1951; Glasgow: Fount Paperbacks, 1979) p. 10.

12. Rainer Maria Rilke, *Sonnets to Orpheus*, with English translations by C. F. MacIntyre (Berkeley and Los Angeles: University of California Press, 1960) p. 6.

13. *The New Jerusalem Bible, Reader's Edition* (New York: Doubleday, 1989, 1990) Genesis, 3:21–22, p. 7.

14. Robert Graves and Raphael Patai, *Hebrew Myths—The Book of Genesis*, (New York: Greenwich House, distributed by Crown Publishers Inc., New York, 1983) p. 77.

15. E. R. Dodds, *The Greeks and the Irrational* (London: University of California Press Ltd., 1951) p. 139.

16. R. H. Tawney, *Religion and the Rise of Capitalism* (New York: Penguin Books Ltd., 1938) p. 111.

17. Friedrich Heer, *The Intellectual History of Europe, Volume II, The Counter-Reformation to 1945* (London: Anchor Books, 1968) Chap. 16, pp. 89–93.

18. Tobias Danzig, *Number: The Language of Science, Fourth Edition— Revised And Augmented* (New York, London, Toronto, Sydney, Singapore: The Free Press, 1954) p. 19 and p. 35.

19. Arthur Waley, *The Way and Its Power—A Study of the Tao Te Ching and Its Place in Chinese Thought* (New York: Grove Press Inc., 1958) p. 155.

20. Compiled by Paul Reps, *Zen Flesh, Zen Bones—A Collection of Zen and Pre-Zen Writings* (Garden City, NY: Anchor Books, Doubleday & Company Inc., 1961) p. 5.

21. John D. Barrow, *The Book of Nothing* (London: Jonathan Cape, 2000). The da Vinci quote in Chapter Two, p. 53, is taken from *The Notebook*, translated and edited by E. Macurdy (London: Jonathan Cape,1954) p. 61.

22. Michael Guillen, *Bridges to Infinity—The Human Side of Mathematics* (Los Angeles: Jermya P. Teacher Inc., 1983) p. 190 and p. 60.

23. C. G. Jung, *AION—Researches into the Phenomenology of the Self*, Translated by R. F. C. Hull, Bollingen Series XX, The Collected Works—Volume 9, Part II (Princeton: Princeton University Press, 1969, fifth printing with corrections, 1978) p. 3.

24. William Shakespeare, *The Tempest* (New York and Scarborough, Ontario: The Signet Classic Shakespeare, New American Library, 1963) I, ii, p. 38.